Learning KORN Shell Fundamentals

Sujata Biswas

Contents

Introduction:

Welcome to "Learning Korn Shell Fundamentals," your comprehensive guide to navigating the Korn shell (KSH) and mastering its essential concepts. In this book, we will explore the foundations of KSH, providing you with the knowledge and skills to confidently use this powerful Unix-like shell.

The Korn shell, commonly known as KSH, was developed by David Korn at Bell Labs in the early 1980s. Building upon the strengths of the Bourne shell (Bash) and the C shell (csh), KSH offers a robust and feature-rich environment for shell interaction and scripting. Its syntax combines elements from various shells, making it both versatile and user-friendly.

In "Learning Korn Shell Fundamentals," we will embark on a journey through the core concepts of KSH. We will cover essential topics such as navigating the file system, working with directories and files, managing processes, and customizing the shell environment. By understanding these fundamental aspects, you will gain a solid foundation for efficiently utilizing the Korn shell.

Throughout this book, we will provide clear explanations, practical examples, and hands-on exercises to reinforce your learning. You will discover how to leverage KSH's powerful features, including variable handling, command substitution, input/output redirection, and shell expansions. With this knowledge, you will be able to streamline your workflows, automate repetitive tasks, and increase your productivity in the Unix-like environment.

While our focus is on mastering the fundamentals of the Korn shell, we believe in keeping the learning process engaging and enjoyable. Along the way, we will share interesting tidbits and insights about the shell's history, notable features, and practical use cases. These fascinating details will not only deepen your understanding but also add a touch of curiosity and appreciation for the Korn shell.

Whether you are a system administrator, developer, or a curious enthusiast, "Learning Korn Shell Fundamentals" is your gateway to unlocking the full potential of KSH. By the end of this book, you will have the confidence and expertise to navigate the Korn shell with ease, harness its capabilities, and optimize your workflow in the Unix-like environment.

Are you ready to embark on this exciting journey into the world of Korn shell fundamentals? Let's dive in and explore the power of the Korn shell together. Let's get started!

Embracing Shell Scripting with Ease

As the specter of automation looms over us, it becomes crucial to arm ourselves with the skills that can safeguard our employment prospects in the years to come. The competition is fierce, with experts in the IT industry expressing concern that up to 60% of IT workers may face job losses. However, even at present, we encounter challenges. With age, the ability to assimilate new skills gradually wanes, a luxury we might have disregarded two decades ago. Nowadays, seasoned professionals are no longer viewed as valuable assets but rather as mere cost units for which companies provide compensation. The prevailing mindset leans towards delegating tasks to fresher faces or interns. Though this may result in a decline in quality, it is essential for us to add value to our roles by acquiring proficiency in new technologies. If our efforts go unrecognized, we can always explore better opportunities elsewhere. Shell Scripting in Linux serves as my response to the automation threat. Let us confront the fears that haunt us and forge ahead. I am confident that with enhanced skills and an improved quality of life for our families, we can ride this so-called wave of automation.

Intended Audience:

Ideally, you should possess some prior experience navigating your way around Linux or other comparable operating systems. The objective is to elevate your scripting skills to a point where you can seamlessly transition to scripting/programming languages like Python, TCL/TK. This is not the culmination but rather the initiation of your learning journey. Certain concepts will be reiterated throughout the book, aiming to ensure your comprehension and establish a robust groundwork.

Chapter 1: Exploring Linux Fundamentals

What is KORN Shell (KSH)?

KSH, short for Korn Shell, serves as an alternative shell available in various operating systems, including Linux and Mint. Renowned for its versatility and robust scripting capabilities, KSH empowers users to harness the full potential of their Linux environments with confidence and efficiency.

By mastering KSH scripting, you will gain a skill set that transcends operating systems, enabling seamless adaptation of your scripts across different platforms. KSH enjoys widespread usage and compatibility, making it a valuable tool for administrators, developers, and enthusiasts alike.

At the core of your Linux operating system resides the kernel, representing the very essence of Linux itself. Acting as a crucial intermediary between users and the underlying hardware components, the kernel establishes an abstraction layer that facilitates smooth and secure interactions with the system.

The shell, encompassing the kernel, provides users like yourself with a powerful interface to navigate and manipulate the Linux environment. With its extensive repertoire of commands, utilities, and scripting capabilities, the shell becomes your gateway to unleashing the full potential of Linux.

Whether connecting to an Ubuntu/Linux system through the secure channels of SSH or the traditional method of Telnet, you will be greeted by the familiar shell prompt, eagerly awaiting your instructions.

$

This humble prompt symbolizes the gateway to a realm of limitless possibilities and untapped potential. It invites you to embark on a journey of discovery, where your curiosity and ingenuity can flourish.

Now, let us embark on this adventure together. Enter the following command:

$ cat /etc/issue

As you execute this command, a window into the heart of your system opens. The "cat" command, a trusted companion in the Linux realm, reveals the contents of the revered "issue" file, offering insights into the identity of your Ubuntu operating system.

Ubuntu 20.04.1 LTS \n \l

Embrace the revelation of progress and innovation. Ubuntu 20.04, a testament to relentless advancement, combines cutting-edge features with steadfast stability. The LTS designation, representing Long Term Support, ensures enduring reliability and extended assistance throughout your Linux journey.

With this newfound knowledge, we stand on the cusp of a new era, brimming with possibilities and opportunities. Let us delve into the vast sea of Linux knowledge, driven by the spirit of exploration and fueled by our shared passion for unlocking the true potential of this remarkable operating system.

To check if your shell is Korn shell (KSH), you can enter the following command:

$ echo $SHELL

$ echo $SHELL

/bin/ksh

The echo command displays the value of the environment variable SHELL. Variables are placeholders in memory that contain a value. In this case, the value is /bin/ksh. The first / represents the root, bin is a directory, and ksh is the executable. Since the entire path is presented from the root, it is referred to as an absolute path.

What are streams?

You must understand or at least review streams. In Ubuntu/Linux, there are three streams:

- Input: What you type on the shell prompt, also known as stdin.
- Output: What the shell returns to you, also known as stdout.
- Error: The error message the shell returns to you, also known as stderr.

Streams are numerically represented as follows:

- stdin: 0
- stdout: 1
- stderr: 2

Note: Streams are an important concept.

Let's enter a command to check the system level we are in. The command we use is who -r, which is the input stream.

$ who -r

run-level 5 2023-05-21 10:30

"run-level 5 2023-05-21 10:30" is the output stream.

The error message 2 (stderr) is useful in shell scripting. In many scripts, we handle true and false conditions. Suppose there is a script that should display an error message like "This command failed to run" when encountering an error. However, you do not want the error message thrown by the script to appear on the standard output (screen). It is better to redirect the error message to a special location called **/dev/null**. You will learn more about redirection in the next section.

Performing **ls -l** on a non-existent file:

$ ls -l nofile.txt

ls: cannot access 'nofile.txt': No such file or directory

Suppose this error message is irrelevant because you want to provide your own error message. What should you do? Remember, there are many cases where you want a condition to fail as well.

$ ls -l nofile.txt 2>/dev/null

$

This means that in case of an error, the error message (signified by 2) should be redirected to the /dev/null file (and not displayed on the standard output or screen).

If the error message is something you need for future reference, such as system logs, you can redirect the error message to a file.

$ ls -l nofile.txt 2> error.log

#Blank next line

$

$ cat error.log

ls: cannot access 'nofile.txt': No such file or directory

What is Redirection?

Redirection is the process of capturing and redirecting command output to a file instead of displaying it on the screen.

$ who -u

peter tty7 2023-05-22 09:45 old 1423 (:0)

bobbydeb pts/19 2023-05-22 09:50 . 17890 (192.168.1.2)

The who command with the -u option displays the output on the screen.

who -u #<- STDIN

⍰

The output or STDOUT is:

peter tty7 2023-05-22 09:45 old 1423 (:0)

bobbydeb pts/19 2023-05-22 09:50 . 17890 (192.168.1.2)

The standard output can be redirected to various destinations, such as a file or a printer. To redirect the output of who -u to a file, we use the > symbol followed by the file name. This way, the output is not displayed on the screen but is instead saved in the specified file.

$ who -u > /tmp/userslist

$

Notice that there is no response from the shell. The output is redirected to a file called userslist (or any preferred name) in the /tmp directory at the root (/). To check the contents of userslist, we use the cat command along with the absolute path to the file.

cat /tmp/userslist

$ cat /tmp/userslist

peter tty7 2023-05-22 09:45 old 1423 (:0)

bobbydeb pts/19 2023-05-22 09:50 . 17890 (192.168.1.2)

Note: It is not necessary to have the userslist file beforehand. If it does not exist, it will be created. If it already exists, the previous data will be overwritten. To append content instead, use >> instead of >.

For example, let's redirect the output of who -r to the userslist file.

$ who -r >> /tmp/userslist

Tip: Take note of the third line.

$ cat /tmp/userslist

peter tty7 2023-05-22 09:45 (:0)

bobbydeb pts/19 2023-05-22 09:50 (192.168.1.2)

In Ubuntu/Linux, everything is treated as a file, including regular files and directories. We can distinguish between these two file types by their permissions.

To examine the contents of a directory, we can use the ls -l command. Directories can contain subdirectories and files. Focus on the first column of the output and mentally divide what you see into four sections in a ratio of 1:3:3:3.

$ ls -l

total 16

drwxrwxr-x 2 bobbydeb bobbydeb 4096 May 23 10:30 testDIR

-rw-rw-r-- 1 bobbydeb bobbydeb 0 May 23 10:30 testFILE

Identifying a directory and its permissions:

drwxrwxr-x 2 bobbydeb bobbydeb 4096 May 23 10:30 testDIR

d indicates a directory. Therefore, testDIR is a directory. If it were a - (dash), it would represent a file. Now, let's break down the next nine characters:

- rwx: The owner, bobbydeb, has read/write/execute permissions.
- rwx: The group, bobbydeb, has read/write/execute permissions.
- r-x: The rest of the world has read and execute permissions.

Note: In this example, the username and group name are the same. This is a default behavior where Linux creates the same username and group name.

Identifying file permissions:

-rw-rw-r-- 1 bobbydeb bobbydeb 0 May 23 10:30 testFILE

-    indicates that it is a file.
- rw-: The owner, bobbydeb, has read/write permissions.
- rw-: The group, bobbydeb, has read/write permissions.
- r--: The rest of the world has only read permission.

It is essential to provide the file's owner with execute permission to run bash script files. You can use the chmod command for this purpose.

Before applying **chmod**, let's observe the permissions for the file testFILE:

-rw-rw-r-- 1 bobbydeb bobbydeb 0 May 23 10:30 testFILE

We will use the chmod command with the u, +, and x operators to "give" (add) the owner, bobbydeb, execute permission denoted by x.

$ chmod u+x testFILE

Note: Run the command chmod u+x <filename.sh> before executing your scripts.

Now, let's perform ls -l on testFILE and observe the difference.

$ ls -l testFILE

-rwxrw-r-- 1 bobbydeb bobbydeb 0 May 23 10:30 testFILE

Tip: To check if a command executed successfully or not, examine the value of the built-in variable: echo $?. This is known as the EXIT STATUS. Any value other than zero indicates an unsuccessful preceding command.

```
$ echo $?
0
```

What are Variables?

A variable in Korn shell (KSH) holds a value that can be changed during script execution. It is important to note that a variable is temporary and should not be confused with a file, which resides on the hard disk.

To define a variable, you can use the following syntax:

$ Example=Ubun2022

To check the value of the variable "Example," use the command:

$ echo $Example

Note: The initial "$" is the command prompt.

In this example, the variable "Example" has the value "Ubun2022," representing a remote system. Let's consider a scenario where a client application relies on the variable "Example" to determine the name of the remote system for specific services. Suppose the machine "Ubun2022" experiences a hardware breakdown, and you have prepared a new remote server as a replacement.

To make the client application work with the new value, change the value of the "Example" variable:

$ Example=Ubun2024

Now, the client application functions properly with the updated value.

If you need to remove the value assigned to a variable, you can use the unset command:

$ unset Example

To perform mathematical expressions with variables, you can assign a number to the variable using a different format:

$ num=100

$ echo $((num))

The value will still be 100, but this construct allows you to perform mathematical calculations using the variable. For example:

$ echo $((num + 300))

400

Variables are also reusable. Here's an example: We define a variable called "filenames" with the values "filename1 filename2 filename3 filename4 filename5." To ensure the shell treats it as a single string, use double quotes. Note that even whitespace holds significance to the shell, but double quotes negate its meaning, so they must be used. The shell expects a single word for the variable value.

$ filenames="filename1 filename2 filename3 filename4 filename5"

$ echo $filenames

filename1 filename2 filename3 filename4 filename5

Note: Use the touch command to create files using the values stored in the "filenames" variable.

$ touch $filenames

Verify using the ls command:

$ ls filename*

filename1 filename2 filename3 filename4 filename5

Hence, this variable "filenames" can be used across the system to create the corresponding files. There is no need to remember the filenames individually; just remember the variable name.

Tip: Variables cannot start with a number. This applies to other scripting and programming languages as well. If you attempt to assign a variable starting with a number, such as "99," an error will occur:

$ 99=hello

99=hello: command not found

Chapter 2: Local Variables versus Environment Variables

Double or Single Quotes?

In Korn shell (KSH), it is essential to understand the differences between double and single quotes, along with other related topics. Let's explore these concepts further.

Setting a Variable's Value:

To begin, let's assign the value of the variable "abc" as 5:

$ abc=5

Displaying Variable Values:

To display the value of the variable "abc," we can use the echo command:

$ echo $abc
5

Variable Expansion:

By default, the shell performs variable expansion, even when using double quotes. For example:

$ echo "$abc"

The output will still be 5, as the shell expands the variable.

Preserving Text with Single Quotes:

When enclosing the variable "abc" in single quotes, variable expansion is not performed. This allows us to preserve the literal text:

$ echo '$abc'

$abc

It's important to note that single quotes and double quotes may appear visually different due to formatting.

Local Variables versus Environment Variables:

In KSH scripting, it is crucial to distinguish between local variables and environment variables.

Local Variables (Shell Variables):

Local variables are applicable only to the current shell instance. When a local variable is defined, such as the variable "height" with a value of 5, it exists within that particular shell instance. However, if we open another instance of the shell using the bash command, the value of the local variable "height" will be empty:

$ height=5

$ echo $height

5

$ ksh # Opening another shell instance

$ echo $height

$

To convert a local variable into an environment variable, we can use the export command. Let's first verify the existence of the local variable "height" and its value:

$ echo $height

5

To make "height" an environment variable, we export it:

$ export height

Now, if we open another instance of the shell and check the value of the "height" variable, we will see that it has been inherited:

$ ksh

$ echo $height

5

Brace Expansions for Variables:

Administrators often use brace expansions to manipulate filenames or perform repetitive operations. For instance, we can copy files with similar names using brace expansions:

$ ls

backup helloA helloB helloC helloD

$ cp hello{A,B,C,D} backup/

This example copies files "helloA," "helloB," "helloC," and "helloD" to the "backup" directory. Similarly, we can achieve the same result using numerical expansions:

```
$ cp hello{A..D} backup/
```

This expands to "helloA," "helloB," "helloC," and "helloD" as well.

Performing Mathematical Calculations:

Korn shell allows us to perform mathematical calculations using brackets. For example:

```
$ echo $((78 * 78))
6084
```

We can assign the result of the calculation to a variable, such as "multiply":

```
$ multiply=$((78 * 78))
$ echo $multiply
6084
```

Command Substitutions:

Command substitution is a crucial concept in KSH scripting. The syntax is as follows:

```
$ variable=$(command)
```

Or

```
$ variable=command (using backticks, not single quotes)
```

For example, we can obtain disk space information using command substitution:

$ echo "The disk space is $(du -sk)"

Consider another example where we extract specific information from the output of the uname -a command using awk:

$ uname -a

Linux linuxmachine 4.4.0-78-generic #99-Ubuntu SMP Thu Apr 27 15:29:09 UTC 2023 x86_64 x86_64 x86_64 GNU/Linux

- $1 - Linux is the First Column
- $2 - linuxmachine is the Second Column

Subsequently, the separators are ever-changing, so the syntax of the awk command will change too. This is a rudimentary introduction to awk, which is a scripting language as well.

$ echo "The operating system is $(uname -a | awk '{print $1}')"

The operating system is Linux #Output

Command substitutions have a special role in shell scripting as they allow us to capture command outputs for further processing. It is crucial to understand and master this sub-topic. In the previous command line, the output of `uname -a | awk '{print $1}'` is assigned as the value to a variable.

Chapter 3: Customizing Your Environment

In the Korn Shell (ksh), you can customize your environment by modifying certain configuration files. These files define system-wide and personal settings to tailor your shell experience. Let's explore how you can customize your Korn Shell environment.

System-wide Settings:

The main system-wide configuration file in Korn Shell is the .profile file. It resides in the /etc directory and contains commands that apply to all users on the system. You can edit this file to set global environment variables and define system-wide aliases and functions.

To modify the system-wide settings, open the **.profile** file with a text editor of your choice and make the desired changes. For example, you can set the PATH variable to include additional directories:

PATH="$HOME/bin:$HOME/.local/bin:$PATH"

Save the changes to the .profile file. The modified settings will take effect the next time you log in or start a new shell session.

Personal Settings:

For personal customizations, you can use the .kshrc file in your home directory. This file is specific to your user account and allows you to define personal aliases, functions, and other settings.

To customize your personal environment, open the .kshrc file with a text editor and add your desired configurations. For example, you can define aliases for frequently used commands:

```
alias ll='ls -alF'

alias la='ls -A'

alias l='ls -CF'
```

Save the changes to the **.kshrc** file. These customizations will be applied whenever you start a new Korn Shell session.

Note: Some systems may use the .profile file for personal settings instead of the .kshrc file. In such cases, make sure to modify the appropriate file based on your system configuration.

Remember to log out and log back in or start a new shell session for the changes to take effect. Your Korn Shell environment will now reflect your customizations, making your shell experience more tailored to your needs.

Please note that the specific file names and file locations may vary based on your Korn Shell implementation and system configuration.

Chapter 4 : Shell Features

Command Structure

The command structure followed by Linux is

command agrument1 arugument2

For example, if we want to rename a file called hello to bye. The command is:

$ mv hello bye

mv is a command, from the shell scripting point it can also be the argument 0 (Zero), hello is the first argument while bye is the second argument.

Command options

For example, we want to see all the hidden files in a directory; the command is:

$ ls -a

While ls is the command, -a is an option.

⍰

What is the Path Variable?

The Path is an important variable. If Path variable is absent, you would not be able to run any commands on the command line. It is a variable that the Shell looks into to execute the binaries that you have typed on the prompt. The value of the Path variable is a list of directories delimited by a colon.

To look the value of the path variable (or any variable for that matter), type

$echo $PATH

/usr/lib64/qt-3.3/bin:/usr/local/bin:/bin:/usr/sbin:/sbin

Chapter 5: Exit Status with AND and OR operators

Linux shell offers exit status for you to know whether your last command is successful or not. The exit status of ZERO means your command has executed successfully, while any NON-ZERO value from 1 to 255 indicates that your command is unsuccessful.

Let us create two files called test1 and test2 using the touch command. When you enter touch command followed by a file name, it creates a new file, if the file does not exist. However, if the file exists, the modification time of the file is changed. Test this using ls -l command.

$ touch test1

If now, you do echo $?, you see a Zero in the output. The $? is a special variable that stores the exit status of the preceding command.

Now type:

$ touch TYPE2

Since Linux is case sensitive, the TYPE2 file is treated differently. However, we have not yet created the TEST2 file.

$ ls TEST2

ls: cannot access TEST2: No such file or directory

You get an error message. Now enter, echo $?

What do you see? You see a NON-ZERO value. In Ubuntu, you may see 2 while in Centos you may see 127. All you need to know is that you have got a NON-ZERO value indicating that the command was unsuccessful.

Most of Linux commands, even built-in binaries, would have exit status in their code. In fact, most of the commands have a section for Exit status in their manual (use the man command followed by the command, like $ man ls) pages.

The AND operator is symbolized by the && on Linux.

Syntax:

command_1 && command_2

Here, command_2 executes when if command_1 successfully executes.

How does the Shell know the first command was successful?

Read the $? Variable and check if the exit value is ZERO. If command_1 is not successful, command_2 does not execute.

Steps:

Create a file using cat > <filename>

cat > exam1

Start typing content and enter Control + d .

$cat exam1

$ls exam1 && cat exam1

$ ls exam1 && cat exam1

exam1

Hello, My name is John

In OR operator, the second command executes only if the first command returns failure or Non-ZERO exit status. The OR operator is symbolized with

|| .

Chapter 6: Managing Processes in Korn Shell

In a Korn shell environment, managing processes is a crucial aspect of controlling your tasks. Understanding how to view, control, and manipulate these processes is essential for effective shell utilization. In this chapter, we will delve into the various commands and techniques used for process management in the Korn shell.

Understanding Processes

Every command you execute on the Korn shell initiates a process. These processes can either run in the foreground, capturing your terminal's focus, or in the background, allowing you to continue other tasks on the terminal.

Viewing Processes

The ps command provides a snapshot of the current processes. To view your processes, simply type:

$ ps

This command displays the PID (Process ID), TTY (terminal type), TIME (CPU time), and CMD (command).

Running Processes in the Background

In Korn shell, to run a process in the background, you append an ampersand (&) to the end of the command. For example, if we wish to run the sleep command for 30 seconds in the background:

$ sleep 30 &

Now, the sleep command runs in the background, freeing up your terminal for other tasks.

Bringing a Background Process to the Foreground

To bring a background process to the foreground, use the fg command followed by the job number. For instance:

```
$ fg %1
```

This command brings job number 1 to the foreground.

8.6 Pausing a Process

If you need to momentarily stop a process without completely terminating it, you can use the kill command with the -STOP signal and the process's PID:

```
$ kill -STOP <PID>
```

This command pauses the execution of the process with the specified PID.

Resuming a Paused Process

To resume a paused process, use the kill command with the -CONT signal followed by the PID:

```
$ kill -CONT <PID>
```

This command resumes the execution of the specified process.

Terminating a Process

To terminate a process, the kill command can be employed with the process's PID:

```
$ kill <PID>
```

This sends a termination signal to the specified process, effectively ending it.

Understanding how to manage processes is fundamental in the Korn shell environment. The ability to view, control, and manipulate processes effectively allows you to manage your tasks efficiently, maximize your productivity, and avoid potential mishaps. As always, practice caution when manipulating processes, especially when using the kill command, to avoid unintended termination or disruption of processes.

Remember, the Korn shell, like many other Unix environments, is a potent tool. Its effectiveness, however, relies heavily on your understanding and command of its diverse features. As you continue your journey, take time to explore and master these process management skills. They will form a significant part of your Korn shell prowess

Chapter 7: Shared Libraries and LD_LIBRARY_PATH in Korn Shell

Understanding Shared Libraries

Shared Libraries are a collection of functions or routines used by various applications. Instead of these functions being replicated in every program, they are stored in a common place, a shared library. This practice saves memory, aids in code reuse, and simplifies application development and maintenance.

Role of Shared Libraries in Korn Shell

In Korn Shell, shared libraries play a pivotal role. When a program is launched, the loader part of the operating system seeks these shared libraries to successfully execute the program. In Korn shell scripting, shared libraries allow scripts to use precompiled functions, creating efficient and robust scripts.

LD_LIBRARY_PATH Environment Variable

The LD_LIBRARY_PATH environment variable is critical in managing shared libraries. It contains a colon-separated list of directories that the loader will look into to find the shared libraries. If a shared library is present in one of the directories listed in the LD_LIBRARY_PATH, it will be accessible to the loader.

To view the current LD_LIBRARY_PATH, use the echo command:

$ echo $LD_LIBRARY_PATH

Modifying the LD_LIBRARY_PATH

To add a new directory to the LD_LIBRARY_PATH, use the export command. For instance, to add /usr/local/my_lib to the LD_LIBRARY_PATH:

$ export LD_LIBRARY_PATH=$LD_LIBRARY_PATH:/usr/local/my_lib

This command appends the new directory to the existing LD_LIBRARY_PATH. Be sure to include the existing LD_LIBRARY_PATH in the command to avoid overwriting the current list.

Troubleshooting with LD_LIBRARY_PATH

Should an application fail to run due to a missing shared library, adjusting the LD_LIBRARY_PATH can often resolve the issue. Add the directory containing the needed shared library to the LD_LIBRARY_PATH, and the loader will be able to find it.

Importance of Managing LD_LIBRARY_PATH

Correctly managing your LD_LIBRARY_PATH is essential for system stability and security. Careless modifications can create conflicts between libraries, leading to application instability, or expose your system to security risks. Always ensure the directories you add are reliable and necessary.

Understanding shared libraries and the role of the LD_LIBRARY_PATH is essential when working in the Korn shell environment. It not only aids in efficient scripting but also in troubleshooting applications. With the mastery of shared libraries management, your proficiency in the Korn shell environment deepens, making you a more competent and confident user.

Chapter 8: Using X11 in the Korn Shell Environment

The X Window System, or X11, is a powerful tool in the world of Unix and Linux. It is an open-source system that provides the basic framework for a graphical user interface (GUI). Despite the growing prevalence of modern graphical desktop environments, having a fundamental understanding of X11 remains crucial for any serious Linux user.

In this chapter, we will delve into the application of X11 in a Korn shell environment. As we journey through, we will find out how X11 intertwines with shell scripting and understand its relevance in the modern Unix-like systems.

Understanding X11

X11 serves as a bridge between the hardware and the user's interactions in a graphical environment. It defines a protocol by which client programs can interact with the display server to produce the graphical output on your screen.

Starting X11

The X11 environment can be initiated with the startx command. However, it is important to remember that X11 uses a lot of system resources. Therefore, it is usually used only when a graphical interface is necessary for tasks such as managing multiple window systems or manipulating graphical data.

Interfacing with X11 in Korn Shell

The integration of X11 with Korn shell scripting opens up an array of possibilities. This combination allows us to create scripts that can interact with graphical environments, gather input from users in a visually engaging way, and even automate graphical tasks.

Creating GUIs with Zenity in Korn Shell

Zenity is a handy tool that lets you create graphical dialog boxes in shell scripts. It extends the interaction of shell scripts with users beyond the terminal, making it more user-friendly. Here's a simple example of a Zenity dialog box in a Korn shell script:

```ksh
#!/usr/bin/ksh
name=$(zenity --entry --text "Please enter your name")
zenity --info --text "Hello, $name!"
```

This script first prompts the user to enter their name, and then it displays a greeting message.

Automating X11 with xdotool

Another powerful tool that can be used in Korn shell scripting is xdotool. This command-line X11 automation tool allows your script to programmatically (and physically) type, move the mouse, click, and more. Here's an example:

```ksh
#!/usr/bin/ksh
xdotool mousemove 300 300
```

This script will move the mouse cursor to the coordinates (300,300) on your screen.

Using xclip for Clipboard Access

The xclip command is a useful tool for interfacing with the X11 clipboard. This can be extremely useful for scripts that need to copy or paste text. Here's a simple example:

```ksh
#!/usr/bin/ksh
echo "Hello, Korn Shell!" | xclip -selection clipboard
```

This script will copy the text "Hello, Korn Shell!" to your clipboard.

The integration of X11 and the Korn shell creates a potent combination that can elevate your scripts' capabilities, allowing them to interact with graphical user interfaces and manage window systems. From automating tedious graphical tasks to creating user-friendly dialog boxes, the applications are boundless.

The examples and tools provided in this chapter should act as a steppingstone into the vast possibilities of using X11 in a Korn shell environment. As you continue exploring, you will uncover even more ways to apply these concepts in your shell scripting journey

Chapter 9: Using OpenGL in the Korn Shell Environment

OpenGL (Open Graphics Library) is a cross-language, cross-platform application programming interface (API) for rendering 2D and 3D vector graphics. The API is typically used to interact with a GPU, to achieve hardware-accelerated rendering. In this subchapter, we'll explore how to use OpenGL within the Korn shell environment and how to update your video driver with the latest OpenGL engine.

Understanding OpenGL in the Unix Environment

In the Unix environment, OpenGL is widely used for tasks that require 2D and 3D graphics rendering. The Unix implementation of OpenGL typically uses GLX (OpenGL Extension to the X Window System) or EGL (Embedded-Systems Graphics Library) to provide the necessary interface between OpenGL and the windowing system.

Using OpenGL in Korn Shell

In a shell environment, OpenGL is typically not directly invoked. Instead, it's used as a library with languages like C++, Python, or Java. However, you can create Korn shell scripts to compile and run programs that use OpenGL.

Here's a basic example:

```
#!/usr/bin/ksh

g++ -o my_program my_program.cpp -lGL -lGLU -lglut

./my_program
```

This script will compile my_program.cpp (which should include OpenGL code) and then run the compiled program.

Updating the Video Driver for the Latest OpenGL Engine

Updating your video driver to accommodate the latest OpenGL engine involves a few steps that are generally done on the command line, and thus can be automated with Korn shell. Please note that the exact steps may vary depending on the specific Linux distribution and the video card you are using.

Identify your graphics card: First, you need to know the specifics of your graphics card. You can do this using the **lspci** command:

```
#!/usr/bin/ksh
lspci | grep -i --color 'vga\|3d\|2d'
```

Download the latest driver: Based on the graphics card details, go to the official website of your graphics card manufacturer (Nvidia, AMD, Intel, etc.) and download the appropriate latest driver that supports the latest OpenGL.

Install the driver: Once the driver is downloaded, you can install it using the package manager for your distribution (apt, yum, dnf, zypper, etc.). The following script assumes an Ubuntu-based distribution and a .deb package:

```
#!/usr/bin/ksh
sudo dpkg -i /path/to/your/driver.deb
```

Verify the installation: After the installation is complete, you can verify the OpenGL version using the glxinfo command:

```
#!/usr/bin/ksh
glxinfo | grep "OpenGL version"
```

This command will output the OpenGL version currently in use by your system, confirming the successful installation of your new driver.

While Korn shell scripts aren't typically used to write OpenGL code directly, they are incredibly useful for automating the compilation and execution of OpenGL programs, as well as for managing and updating OpenGL drivers. Keep in mind that the specific details may vary based on your system configuration, but the principles remain the same.